CHEWING THE FAT

CHEWING THE FAT
a collection of poems

Edited by Cetywa Powell

Underground Voices
www.undergroundvoices.com
2009

Chewing The Fat: a collection of poems

Copyright © 2009 by Cetywa Powell

All rights reserved. No part of this book may be used or reproduced by any
means, graphic, electronic, or mechanical, including photocopying, recording,
taping or by any information storage retrieval system without the written
permission of the publisher.

CONTENTS
i.
the written word disguised as truth

John Sweet
the written word disguised as truth
memory (2)
in a room, blindly
a darker room
north, past dryden, past cortland

Michael Shorb
photograph taken at a lynching (1919)
chilling with dictators

Carol Carpenter
on reconnaissance

Scott Wannberg
the war
rumors of life

Daryl Horton
i think I know what it feels like to…

ii.
natural selection

John Macker
an underwebbing of customary magic
indian summer
the roaring stillness across open ground
call me the doc holliday of language

S.A. Griffin
natural selection
there is
the meeting minutes of the homeless, mad & otherwise
clinically depressed
god, a night light in eternity

John Dorsey
peter pan at 45
poem for a toothless lion
blues for a 9 millimeter ghosttown
i like hotels

iii.
habits

Tony O'Neill
iris circle, again

Ron D'Alena
on alamitos hill

R.C. Edrington
habits
pornographic novel
pretty little mess

Debbie Kirk
word factory
behind me now

iv.
stories to tell

Dennis Cruz
i open myself up
i never told you before, but...

James Babbs
disturbing the light
heavy on my mind
jack and coffee and the rain coming down

Richard Wink
again over and over

D.B. Cox
stories to tell
searching for the door
friday night in the drunk tank
the ward
dust-off

Robert Plath
one for Li Po

Cynthia Ruth Lewis
diluted
last words
going by feel

Lyn Lifshin
like some lies we tell ourselves
the other fathers
my father's wallet
september 23rd, 1996
almost the way she stood in the bathroom with the door
locked at two

Lafayette Wattles
death comes in smallness
something more

Michele Leavitt
seven to life

v.
again over and over

Greg Scharf
one for the metaphysicians, or...
i love you in other words
i wanted to write something nice about love but ended up writing this instead

Keith Niles
it's just me, mid-madness
the lows of Vegas

Karl Koweski
they call me Captain Gringo
art and commerce

M.K. Chavez
Americana

Joseph Veronneau
roadside
unspoken
at the dinner table

Nathan A. Baker
fathers and sons
an urn of ashes

Mather Schneider
bananas
scooter

John Grochalski
one of the best
lessons from a master
success

Duncan Fankboner
in the middle of the last century
not the buddha

J.J. Campbell
the bullets of ignorance
a war of attrition

Cortney Davis
hooked up
first night at the cheap hotel

The written word

John Sweet

The written word disguised as truth

the women are raped
silently beneath a blue sky
in rooms with or without windows

this is always a part of
someone's history

the smell of burning flesh and the
photographs of the slaughtered and
in the here and now i am
cupping your breasts in my
sweatslicked hands

i am naming the stars and
blessing the spaces between them
and there is a day where i
realize i will no longer live forever

where my son
will see for the first time
the man i truly am
and turn away in shame

there are pages in history that
cannot be rewritten
but i have yet to see one

i include my own life here

the events that actually happened
and the ways they were changed in
                the retelling
and i am no different from any of you

about this much
at least
i can be honest

it costs me nothing to
point out
that we will all drown together

John Sweet

Memory

thinking last night that
i was twenty two and that
you were still alive
and then waking up to the sound
of rain and the baby crying

sitting in a dark room
measuring the distance from
the bridge to the train tracks below

considering the simplicity of cancer

of someone being dropped
naked and screaming
almost fifty feet
and the way you cried as i got in the car
and drove away

the weight of the phone for
the next two weeks
and then months and then years

the ghost of kay sage
and the memory of gorky

the beauty of the space
between them

and there is a place where
the mountains pull apart and
the road seems to almost
have direction

there are the trailer parks
and the cars rusting on blocks
and the empty buildings
without purpose

the mother who drinks drano
on her kitchen floor
and the one who murders her
oldest daughter

walls filled with fading pictures

always more and
always more of the same

names and faces and
minor acts of violence

the news of a war that can't be won

the president's smile as he
grows fat on the meat of
butchered children and the way
i sat up in bed with a name i
hadn't spoken in fifteen years
falling from my lips

the sounds the house made
around me

all of the ways
in which silence isn't

John Sweet

In a room, blindly

Not lies, really,
but truths that can't be proven.

The ghosts of Aztecs,
of Incas.

Parking lots.

Palaces.

Man rolls the dice to see which of
the children will starve,
and then the bomb goes off.

Seventeen dead, blood everywhere,
the pews of the church on fire.

The runoff from the mill
dumped into the river.

Close your eyes and picture it.

The first time we met and then,
two years later,
the first time we made love.

Oceans on every side of us,
wars to the south,
to the east,
and I told you you were beautiful.

Had no words beyond that,
only abstractions.

Only need.

Thirty seven years old and
suddenly no longer blind and,
in the mountains,
the killers were making new plans.

In town,
the streetlights were coming on.

It seemed almost possible
we would find our way home.

John Sweet

A darker room

not the storm
but the waiting

pale yellow sunlight
falling from a dirty silver sky
and the shadows of branches

the idea of starvation
which should never be confused
with the reality of it

the way you crawl either
towards or away from whoever
says they love you

no words
only actions

broken glass and
the way it tastes being
forced down your throat

the way your children
see everything

your daughter
pulling away from your touch

the marks on her back

what they finally mean

John Sweet

North, past dryden, past cortland

or the way the sky
refuses to give up its light
in july

the way the disappeared
are forgotten

their faces first
and then their names
and then the fact that they were
ever loved at all

small crosses planted on
the side of the highway and
the way they rot

the way nothing grows
around them but weeds

and not everyone tires of
blaming god for their pain

not every deserving tongue
is cut out

look at you

look at me

all of the addicts that
fill the miles between us

all of the children learning

how to inflict pain or
receive it

at what point
do we tell them that
these are their
only choices?

Michael Shorb

Photograph Taken At a Lynching (1919)

The galling thing's
how proud they seem,
a dozen citizens or more,
crowding into the lens'
purview, some smiling,
some stern or effecting
righteousness, all
seeming to say

'this we have done, and
this the way things will be
in this small river town.'

In the foreground, not even
hanging in air but
crudely strangled, neck
clearly broken, displayed
against an oak tree
like a skinned deer,
the skinny black man,
young, eyes bulging,
capable of some
mistake or violation
of the rules no doubt,
and the all purpose
epitaph:

       this one

got uppity.

Michael Shorb

Chilling With Dictators

After the hard work of
liquidating millions
what's a little relaxation in
expropriated gardens,
rapture in hammocks
with blue distant Alps
languid under skullcaps
of snow?

After the speeches in sports stadiums
billowing cigar smoke of
conference rooms muted
shotgun booms blazing in cellars
fires under the sea there's
no harm in patting the dog or
sliding your hand
        down the blouse
of the mistress
in pigtails

        And the black train
with its load of frozen birds
its kingdom of art treasures and violins
stuck in a snowbank on the Russian front.

While Beria bounces pudgy Svetlana
on his knee Stalin catches up on Gulag
paperwork
    wine in the glasses
catches fire
      Lenin and Hitler
play tennis on the clay
leaping and whirling like blood-

stained schoolboys, their laughter
echoing in the engines of the snow.

Carol Carpenter

On Reconnaissance

I spot one woman's coiffed head
skewered on a fencepost
beside an empty shack.
No body. No extremities.
Just a plastic head in this war zone
jammed onto a rusted metal tube.

I curse whoever
concocted this atrocity,
this violent monstrosity. It could be me
with brown hair, flipped at the end
and querulous eyes exposed
in this mannequin's molded face.

Like me, this dummy occupies a space
someone else chose. Could she be
a warning, a woman
in a morality play
who lost her tongue
spying for the enemy?

I cannot decipher
the coded message painted
in pink sunset on her lips
turned up at the corners
as if she knows the secret
handshake for my safe passage
through this bloody world
where I must wear camouflage
and streak my face with mud.

Scott Wannberg

The War

The War had its grandchildren over for the afternoon
they looked at the scrapbook
smiled, told one another jokes, ate well...
The War told everyone it was going to wear brand new clothes
but if you look close enough
the labels are angrily familiar...
The War knows where to buy food cheap
but good stuff nonetheless...
The War had a drinking problem
but it got smart, joined AA
nothing but coffee now...
The War came over to my apartment this afternoon
to borrow a video
I don't know if I should loan the War any of my things
It usually loses them, forgets to return anything...
The War got on its knees and prayed for more victims
before turning in.
Dear God, the War said, please let me go on and on and on
I am enjoying myself.
The War is getting younger all the time.
Nobody should look that young.
Nobody.

Scott Wannberg

Rumors of Life

Men and women argue about which gender has been
wounded the most.
Law abiding women and men demand their chance at
being outlaws.
Rumors of Life everywhere you hang.
Cities of humans bent on doing good.
Bent humans in cities up to no good.
Bring the flame a little closer.
Let me see your doctor's calling card.
God won't see you unless you make an appointment.
Bring your insurance.
Men and women line each other up on the firing range.
Look at me, they say, and bow toward the comet
that is determined to smash into us.
Men and men too will be coming over soon.
Women and women as well, to follow.
They all come with their pails and shovels.
they all want their time in the big sandbox of love.
Rumors of Life in every corner of the dark hole.
The only true disease tonight is the one of pride,
and what you think you really might turn out to be
when all of it ends.
The wind comes over for tea,
the wind begins to blow its anger.
Watch the faces and the hearts of the men and women
blowing ever so polite
across the barbed wire.
Watch the smiling hit squad
they claim they have good aim.
Keep your fingers crossed,
tell all lies with conviction.
God will see you now.
You may not come out alive.

But God is whittling his knife and
very much wants to take a look into you.

Daryl Horton

I think I know what it feels like to...

Suffer from
Inability to sleep for
Another five hours, please
As if eyelids were stapled, pinned back to forehead
Too much time spent
Searching cracked ceiling paint
Like Alcoholics searching the bottom of bottles for
Solutions to why we struggle,
Struggling to fill
Week long days with
S O M E T H I N G
Other than endless moments of
N O T H I N G like
Man eclipsed by ground hog day.
That's what we call the daily repetitions in WAR
Wake up
Get dressed
Eat chow
Go to work
Eat chow
Shower
Sleep
Repeat all
Only I left out reactions to dangers of being here
But dangers of being here are not what plague our
minds
Monotony broken by dangerous encounters freeing us
for
Fleeting moments of change, from
Our real enemy...time
Becoming once again entangled repeating repetitions of
Free time spent trapped between
The desire to do something you like yet

Too tired to repeat doing what you love
So we lay congealed in
Indecision as
Month 12 in Iraq clanks by like a
1976 Mustang hatch back in need of serious maintenance
And we begin to wonder if prison feels the same.

Natural selection

John Macker

"An Underwebbing Of Customary Magic"

A ride through the homicidal winter
Of January, just this side of the Texas line
Jack's got frostbite
On his big toe on account of
His worn out boots, no shit,
We're in the vanilla center of
A religious white-out, must
Be close to midnight, we're freezing
Shitless & surly as badgers;

I swear, my
Cock's frozen still-life to the inside of
My leg in my britches & my ass
Is frozen like a shaved otter
To my saddle &
To make matter's worse, Jack's got
A bullet hole in his cheek, it lodged in his
Gums, in front of his wisdom teeth
There on the left side if you're looking
At him straight on &
I'll be goddamned if he don't complain
To himself in absolute .44 caliber silence.
The guy's like a fucking Benedictine monk who's
Taken a vow of poverty which is why we
Rustle like we do as well as we do & a vow
Of the zippered mouth, too- most of
Us only go south once in our lives,
Might as well do it with a snowflake's
Worth of quiet dignity.

Suddenly, Jack, bent over his saddle horn
Like a ragged scythe begins speaking, softly,
A bloody cat's paw for a tongue:

"Grasshoppers swarm
through the desert
there are only grasshoppers
Lady
Of Guadalupe
Make my sight clear
Make my breath pure
Make my arm stronger and my fingers tight
Lady Of Guadalupe, lover
Of many make
Me avenge
Them."

The radio tonight will not tell
Of the death of Billy The Kid.
Or Jack Spicer. Will not permit it. Even
With these wounds I mock this travesty of
A storm front birthed with a whimper
In the faraway womb of the Sangres. In blizzards
We do all the singing for the birds.
As a morale boost to Jack I say:
"Stay awake hombre,
let us fake out a frontier-
a poem somebody could hide in with a sheriff's
posse after him-
a poem with no hard corners, no underwebbing
of customary magic ... only a place Billy The Kid
can hide when he shoots people ...   the poem."

In all this distance, who'll recognize my face?

An overwebbing of thick cloud post-
Midnight, low to the ground, surly mist still
Spitting snow, cholla clusters scrape at my
Pant legs, bellicose radio static to the skin
Seemingly everywhere, the humming of
Bare naked wire overhead in the wind, a Texas

Affectation to be sure, just as the thundering hooves
Of barbaric Panhandle justice are meeting their
Doom on the horizontal, faux-arctic prairie.
Where the Comanche
With a sudden infusion of equine
Energy torture & kill upended
American Cadillacs in the name of
Homeland security while leaving
Coyote to his own devices.

In all this distance I recognize his face. The poem.

John Macker

Indian Summer

Autumn as much a notion as it is
warm day, handwritten
red crayon moon
above the canyon
in slow motion, a crisp
yellow leaf afloat in its singularity
flows down a shadowed stream
into the Roaring Fork
is peace

Miles Davis, kind of blue & low
a love potion
alone on my
old turntable
is peace
as peace is inevitably
the wild practice

of listening/
   to a tribe of dry leaves or
waters reflecting currents
of transparent sunlight,
or a raven's wing beat
the allure of pure high country
this time of year, the practice
of the season's
shortening days more
languor than furor;

thinking of war I can't help but
think of immutable total peace
yet some day's farther from
war's cure than cancer-

it's going to take more than a sorcerer,
more than four horsemen,
where common ground isn't killing ground
it'll take more than simple necromancers
or incantations & there will be some
sort of solace
for the torturers,
a place of ballast they can go,
a river
& above the river

trees where
they can shed themselves of such
practices that keep them in the furor
of a common darkness
away from this morning's
October light.

John Macker

The roaring stillness across open ground

I'm kicking up the desert dust with my two dogs
on the kind of dry crisp morning
that draws the blue sky down around
it & everything that exists under it
the hummingbirds
spanish bayonet
the enflamed loose ends of war, the

yellow snakeweed & bahia
blossoms bobbing in the breeze
like rogue stars. The
emergence myths that rise from
the earth in ghost vendettas of
language.
The piney smell of the hike
resuscitates us
mothers us into knowing
these rituals come with the territory-
where we're amazed at the proximity
of faraway war,
its roaring stillness across open ground:

lone rufous hummer
destined for Mexico
last supper of the summer at
our plastic nectar blossom,
controlled burn-colored body hovering:
thinks I'm the chief flower of my species
crisscrosses my Hawaiian shirt like
a bandolier,
signifying a farewell of sorts,
the last of his tribe still this far north
from the Crossing of the Fathers to

the Rio Grande
a thousand heartbeats per minute

miles to go before real peace.

John Macker

Call Me The Doc Holliday Of Language

Of misanthropic scorpions, dust dervishes
Dry rivers
The psilocybin horizon
Diseases of the lung
Have no voice in this outback
Of an era
I witnessed the fall of the South
In Colorado, I heard my disembodied
Voice in the tall pine
Thunderheaded she-rain.
I move from one incandescent
Quick-draw to another seduced
With the knowledge that this
Is more an occult gesture
Than gun hand.

I speak Latin.
I've opened De Vinci's notebook
To where it says The Last Supper
In the dark of the bar
Three fingers of sour mash
I bend over the glowing pages
Like a high priest.

I am the voice of the wasteland,
The wasted, the outgunned, the
Disenfranchised
The black hollyhock
The mockingbird's psychedelic
Soundtrack to the simple act
Of me, riding my pony
Across the movies as a kid.

S.A. Griffin

Natural Selection

Black Flagg had set his mind
to be top dog
in The Washington Manor street gang
thought he was bad
so he put out the word to
Louis Sanchez: "I choose you out."

the interested student body
convened on the San Leandro side
of the Barrett Bridge
after school
eager for the
action

Flagg was meaty
tough & willing
but a bit slow on the
uptake

Louie was
smart
rugged
and cool

the dude was clean:
pegged Farah slacks
boss, black leather Turks curled at the tip
immaculate mohair sweaters tucked up over his
forearms
his blue black hair
always pressed into a perfect
bad boy pomp
blessed with a congenital charm

Louie never messed with anyone
that didn't mess with him first

Like Flagg

who began to shuffle and circle a bit
bobbing & weaving
like he knew the game
anxious to make his mark
and prove himself

Louie held his ground
leaning in a bit
smiling & pointing at his chin
repeating, "C'mon Flagg, right here man.
C'mon… yeah man, let's go… c'mon man…"

Flagg was uneasy
scared
& confused
by Louie's crazy cool

foolishly Flagg finally swallowed
& took the hook
swinging wide and hard

it was over before it began

stealth like a jungle cat
Louie systematically
took Flagg apart
zero to 60
from the top down
in a flurry of dust & ferocious form
that spanned seconds

he never broke a sweat

& looked just as good coming out of the fight
as he did
going in

poor fucking Flagg
the dumb defeated sonofabitch
left disassembled in the dirt
like useless car parts
as everyone walked away
swept up by the godlike declaration of
speed
youth & muscle
that was Louie's
the brief
but curious battle
executed with flawless grace & beauty
no less than the best
of any dance or
music

the rest of us
left of hunger with cryptic wonder
restless inside the green naked glow of our
nascent youth
not knowing
much if anything
at all
yet certain in our
unawareness

the years stretched out before us
like lactating lions
before hungry laughing jackals

patiently waiting to pick off
the weak & the
dumb

S.A. Griffin

There Is

and still the sun screams down
upon this fleetingly sane and wicked monument to
mortality
the machine guns of eternity grind out the days
the nights
fate hammers
down its final verdict
upon humanity somewhere as something breathes itself
into extinction
the humanity we often never had
and many never will
but still believe in
that there is still
time enough for whatever it is
you have yet to accomplish on your
list of things left to do
that more than likely
will never get done
and only remember
that you are not alone
never were
never will be
no matter who or what you think you are
that within the darkest chambers of the heart
there is the possibility of light
that within the biggest tightest asshole
that leaves the biggest foulest footprint upon the blue
blue morning of the
globe
there exists something so small and physically
imperceptible inside that
asshole
with the ability to send that rage tumbling

back into the earth
something renewable
something still with the ability to
unravel government plots
stifle corporate will
unexplain the gods
and cause joy inside this tortured
world of war all the time
there is a flower that can't be stopped
there is laughter that must be heard
there is someone's love song with your eyes inside of it
looking out
there is another moment left before the last
before the next
there is still time for love if you so desire
even if you don't
there is
regardless of what you think or feel or don't
there is

S.A. Griffin

**The Meeting Minutes of the Homeless,
Mad & Otherwise Clinically Depressed**

hopelessly (laughing all the way)
we dialogue over dollar coffee almost daily

the 65 year old guy sleeping on floors for nearly a year
the slightly tilted Korean vet
living in the bushes around the corner for almost as long
the 3rd a recent Yale grad
freezing his ass off in a downtown loft waiting for work
the 4th couch surfer sprung from the womb of this
stylish neighborhood
recovering from a soft stroke some months back

hand rolled cigarettes & caffeine fueled small talk
wrap themselves around precious days
addressing issues far out of anyone's orbit:
warrior presidents next to god the global buck
the anathema & irrelevance of old world theologies
false elections
shrinking budgets & crippling debt
the centuries old exercise of obscene freedom
as practiced upon the free
& the infinite justice of unholy war

we live death
every moment
every day
imagined or not
one foot in front of the other
one leg at a time

the untouchable republic
America, flame thrower of love

dreamers awake
a pale rider on dark horse
approaches full of eyes
armed with a shout
to raise the dead
& will not be
denied

S.A. Griffin

God, a night light in eternity

there from the
beginning
at last
the tease of
infinity
grins

Everything Is All Right
In Time
Even Death

100 miles per hour to nowhere
point blank verse
pain heaped upon pain
thru addiction
or just simply being
available
to the process

the march & mulch of war

burgers & fries
obsessive sex
the opiates of
religion

whatever it is
it will get us all
in the end

pick your poison well
live for it

blossom & burn
inside the sacred unfolding of the
laughing rose

even the sun will lose
its hair & go blind

John Dorsey

Peter Pan at 45

it was January 17th 1968
when you came out   after reading
kerouac   all of that bottled up
macho energy   spent
on free love

"midnight cowboy" was the story
of your life   landing on 42nd street
while joe buck was still a zygote
in search of ginsberg's angry fix
finding hell at dawn   with
greasy fingers

your hat like a crown   strewn
from tattered green felt
should have tipped everyone off
except in the haight   you were
just considered   average

everybody knew about wendy
you jumped out of that window
together   finding paradise
but things got too heavy
and you landed on earth alone

many times they had told
the story of your youth
playing you off   as a
forever boyish oliver twist type

looking in the bathroom mirror
you pondered middle age
with tinkerbell   a withering

drag queen   working the corner
of grant & green   for
cheap Mexican beer   just one
last time

your stomach sloping/sagging
in contrast   to
the sun

you had been a real hustler   once
growing older   but never really growing up
or perhaps it was the other way around
who remembers these things?

As a kid   i
felt cheated
wishing you   back
to neverland   you weren't
that wonderful boy
after all

just a sad
middle aged has been
in
tights

John Dorsey

Poem for a toothless lion

you were a sonnet
in a dark alley
a toothless lion a slow
disease painting a still life of death

when time brought you sunflowers
you piled brick on top of brick
inside your heart
i camped out there
looking for words
with a flashlight and
an open heart
remembering what you always said

dream like you have a gun to your head

i knew a woman
who was pregnant for 32yrs
packed 40hrs into the
first 24 but still
i've never really lived
just watched as the
last embers of rome
flowed through your pen
in little italy

it's just after 5am somewhere
and if i cut
a
box in half that
doesn't make things magical

the walls in this

room grin back at
me with apathy

you told me once
about how they used
to build whole city states
out of poems

how everything you see here
is made out of
the bones of dreams

how having a stiff
drink with lorca meant
you had to write
everything down right away

lately the words just
won't come

the words
to say i love you
like death

a few wks ago
i crossed an arroyo
finding only red earth
and stones i looked for angels bones
inside the skeleton of
a melted typewriter

why is it that
i feel like the
ghost in this relationship?

there's a light in

the corner of the room

i want to reach
for a pen
sing to the dead
in an eternal language of love
to shoot my way out
of dreams

it is after 5am somewhere
and i need this poem
to reach you and
find you well

John Dorsey

Blues for a 9 millimeter ghosttown

on most days you
will find them here
detroit land of the
casual werewolf they
will sing you to
sleep on magic ave.
they say to drink
dark milk wait for
the commentary of shadows
here even the ghosts
carry 9 millimeters through
streets of broken dreams
tucked inside a book
your language has yet
to be written down
you'll see the sun
doesn't shine here god
lost a coin toss
and decided to build
housing projects on the
outskirts of heaven the
earth was hand made
a paradise of masturbation
where the children tell
stories in silence hungry
the dead send their
street sweepers through to
collect your dreams and
gather in a circle
before eating their
                young

John Dorsey

I like hotels

      because you can read hamlet
under a jesus nitelight
      screaming about betrayal
      while eating powdered donuts
sipping black coffee
      listening to phantom sounds of miles davis
on a busted turntable

or dream about mermaids
      dishing out soup
in 1930's oklahoma
      smoldering under the very sun
that would do in john steinbeck

      or fanciful thoughts of ruby slippers
that never seem to fit
      on a honeymoon
in modesto
touring the boone's farm winery
      forgetting all about wanting
to stomp grapes with mae west
      in boneyard alleys

you can forget about that

      I like hotels because the dreams have vacancies

          the kind that don't ask questions

Habits

Tony O'Neill

Iris Circle, Again

I awoke from a nightmare of my own devising
and came back into the one we shared:
it was 4 am and she was next to me
overdosing on cocaine

she shimmied and shook, naked and
smeared brown from the previous night's
frenzied,
compulsive injecting

eyes rolled back into her head
arms twisting at arcane
spastic angles

a sad
bruised
98 pound
St. Vitus

amidst the screaming
and the phone calls
and the ambulance
and the restraints
she looked at me
and said
"Why?
"Why did you let me wake up?"
one sound
above the screams and the
crying and the sirens
still reverberates in my head

the sound of the paramedics

heavy, solid boots
treading on, and crunching underfoot
the remnants
of a life imploded

Ron D'Alena

On Alamitos Hill

1.
Clay Mackey sits on swivel stool,
fishes a Marlboro from shirt pocket,
strikes a match with cold fingers,
lights the cigarette.

The waitress's middle-aged face brightens.
Clay is her only customer.

2.
He sits, shoulders sagging,
elbows hard against Formica countertop,
coffee cup loosely held in left hand.

He looks at the waitress –
belly swollen,
tight.

"Son of a bitch put the bun in the oven,
then run off."

3.
Clay remembers Carrie Lee Keegan:
reclining upon a field of colorful wildflowers,
high atop Alamitos Hill,
next to the cemetery,
spring air swirling with chatty song of common finches.

She had refused to undress – at first.
But he had to have her so he said, "Yeah, I love you."

4.
He looks past the waitress,

to a chrome strip bordering a glass case with empty
shelves.
He notices his reflection –
face gaunt,
a withered apple.

The morning he had left home Carrie Lee Keegan caught
up with him
before he could hitch a ride.

At first she said,
"Please stay with me."
Then she said,
"I hope you die and rot away somewhere by yourself."

The waitress straightens a row of plastic ketchup bottles.

Clay looks out the window at the fog
pulsing red beneath rooftop sign:
24-HOUR GOURMET.

5.
Yesterday he had decided to return home –
to his father's automobile repair business,
to humble himself to Carrie Lee Keegan.
And so he telephoned her to tell her as much.

It was then he discovered she had died
attempting to rid herself
of their baby.

Her family had buried her on
Alamitos Hill,
in the cemetery next to the meadow
of their lovemaking.

6.
Clay steps into the damp,
neon-red fog.
walks through a vacant lot littered with
broken glass,
weeds,
scraps of corrugated tin.

He stops at the edge of the 101,
pulls frayed corduroy jacket against his body,
blows warmth into cupped hands.

The highway: vacant in both directions.
Then the throaty drone of a motor.
Dull headlights appear in the fog.

Clay Mackey steps onto the highway,
curls his hands into fists,
faces the oncoming driver.

The bumper strikes him into a drainage ditch
running parallel to a barbed wire fence.

For a moment he tries to free his limbs from stabbing
barbs.
Then he doesn't move at all.

R.C. Edrington

Habits

We'd duct taped
faded newspapers
to the bedroom windows
& erased the sun

the silence between us
palpable, thick
& black like
fresh tar
on a once familiar
gravel road
we'd never travel again

a long forgot cigarette
burnt itself out
on a crushed
Diet Pepsi can,
the ash bent
& ready to fall
like a timid suicide
perched on
the Golden Gate Bridge

for 3 days
nothing was shared
but a dull rig
& 7 grams
of uncut dope

time itself nothing
but a false restraint
we'd long since escaped
as we sat like

twin Buddhas rotting
on a stained mattress

when you held me
tight in your numb
powdered sleep
I knew you were only
dreaming of someone else,
as was I
both too weak
to break old habits
& embrace the dawn
creeping slow beneath
the thin slice
of the battered
bedroom door

R.C. Edrington

Pornographic Novel

The way a drunken cock
sadly begs for penetration,
she pokes the syringe
up and down the worn veins
in her frail tattooed arm.

From the bedroom window,
I am left alone to witness
the whispering wound of moonlight
bleed shadows thru
cottonwood branches
clinging like black fishnet stockings
to midnights bruised thighs.

Once there was love
which passed between us,
where now there is only silence...
and her love was like
a windowless basement
on a storm raped night,
nothing existed outside
its womb like darkness.
But this shelter has begun to cave
like the veins which scar her arms,
and now I'm trapped
within this tomb-like loneliness
searching for an exit door
that may no longer even exist.

In the alley below,
a vietnam veteran in bell bottom jeans
sips the nectar of muse
from a brown papered bag,

then fades into the rear doorway
of an adult movie house
where for .25 cents he'll receive
enough inspiration
to make a metaphor of his hand.

And I wonder,
if her desire to touch me
will ever again be as strong
as her need for a fix right now,
or will she just continue
to pantomime her emotions
like a seasoned porno star.

R.C. Edrington

Pretty Little Mess

you vampiric little mime
with your sad cliché
of smudged black eyeliner
& charcoal blackened lips,
polished red leather
mini-skirt & bra shines
like cheap plastic
in this forced
terrace moonlight.

I'll write books about
the 3 a.m. nosebleeds
& tissues tossed
like tampons
in your kitchen trash
& the antique
Betty Boop cigarette case
chalky white
with that poorly cut cocaine
you hide beneath
your microwave.

so roll your vacant
23 year old spoiled brat eyes
at my tired life
at my barrio whores & junkies
at my low rent criminal friends,

all you really want
my Prozac numbed
wrist slit Juliet
is to capture me
in your deluxe 3 bedroom

condo cage
as tho I'm some lost
hopeless romantic
poster child
for tortured artist.

an artist I'm not
despite how much
of your dead daddy's cash
you stuff like sluttish fingers
into the front pocket
of my frayed jeans
crumpled like
an old love letter
on your bedroom floor
as I sleep to dream
of somewhere
& someone else.

I am exactly who
& what I am
nothing more-nothing less
but sometimes
when I'm buried deep
inside of you--
my eyes clenched shut
against that stupid
pentagram tattoo stain
between your tender
shoulder blades,
I wonder who
& what exactly
you think you are.

Debbie Kirk

Word Factory

When the words really scream
the kind of scream that makes red drip from the corners
of your mouth...
I thought they had to have been written by a man
carrying the uneven weight
of unrequited love
Swaggering through dark alleyways
with a trench coat on and a flask in hand
contemplating the large exit.

When I read such beautiful words about madness
The madness that doesn't know it exists, and lives
in it's own shadow.
Madness that make some people build gallows,
and others laugh until they can't bleed anymore

I think that they must have been scrawled
on a matchbook by a young woman who is aged only
by the layers of dirt on her face and memories in her
head
A woman whose teeth rattle when she coughs.

So, they took my shoestrings
And gave me something "to calm down a little"
And I'm a little confused for a while
Because I thought this would surely be the place
Where the words would flow like the wine I finished
Without a glass.
But instead of writing words that dance on my tongue
I watch the clock for med time

Then I laugh out loud
As I realize, this is the factory

Where they try to take away your words forever
But they can't get me
Without words, I don't exist
And I'm not that fucking lucky

Debbie Kirk

Behind me now

I play jump rope barefoot
amongst the tossed razors and syringes
and once I used a Ouija board to find out who
he really was
inside of me.
I lost my echo
when I checked the pulse
and found my shadow
when I discovered that wine
came in a box.
I caught a tiger by the toe once,
and his teeth were like the needles
I'd later fall in love with.
My mom would cut my peanut butter sandwiches
into triangles
I would try to invent a potion
that would make me a mermaid.
I could roller skate better than anyone else my age
but when I turned tricks
everyone looked the other way
I used to cheat at cards
against myself
and I still always came up
being a loser.
No one ever told me not to swim in the deep end
and no one told me that I could never be a mermaid.
These things you learn early in life
stick to you
Like the gum my cousin put in my hair
when we all went to Six Flags.
I stood on my sand pail
and tried to hang myself with that jump rope once,
but all I got was a scratched knee

and failure and sadness
that would stay with me forever
as I realized that sometimes there really is no way out.
Prisoners act like prisoners
and I feel like I should be singing the blues
Put shackles around my ankles
and perhaps my behavior would make more sense.
I just wanted you to know
That I still want to be a mermaid
And that jump ropes
Ain't good for a hangin'.

Stories to tell

Dennis Cruz

I never told you before, but...

It was the way you told me...
Like stretching something over
Everything I leaned on
to keep me afloat,
Like pulling it up
and over my head,
Not quite suffocating,
But still
Making the soft
pulling in of air
A struggle.
Something about
the way
you leaned in
and whispered,
Not even secretive
Just...careful
Not to hit
So hard
making me
Too aware,
Of how alone
We had suddenly
become.
It was at that moment
With the quiet pressing
Against us...
And the fear
Passing over
Both our eyes
I converted...
Never questioning
Never looking back

Just this trust
Like a warmth
Then this knowing
Once and forever after
That you would be
The most beautiful
Animal
I would ever
Encounter
In this
Or any other
Lifetime.

Dennis Cruz

I open myself up

The blade just one rusted
Recollection...
I do it right down the middle
The belly splits easily
A leakage dripping down the sides
Like some bad stigmata
But amidst all the stink
Of entrails and gluttony
I find no sign
Of the tapeworm.
I lift flaps of flesh
And ropes of matter
But still...
No sign
And I was so sure
I could feel it moving,
feeding
On the blood
Of all my bad impulses
But if there's no worm
Then what could be
Moving, in there?
After hollowing myself
Completely out...
I become convinced
The worm has died
And I've already
Passed it and I
Make a mental note
To take a closer
Look at what
Passes through
Before I flush it

Into oblivion.
Because without a
Worm
There is only
Me
And that's just
Too much to bear.

James Babbs

Disturbing the Light

sitting here in
the living room watching
the way the sunlight falls
across the floor making
these rectangles of light and
I remember how you
always avoided them
whenever you got up to
go to the bathroom or
the kitchen stepping
carefully over them or
walking around them but
never just going through them and
one day I asked you
why you did this and
you laughed, softly
said you didn't want to
disturb the light and
now you're gone and
I want to run around the room
scream at the top of my lungs and
step into the middle of
all those rectangles so
the light shines on me and
no longer touches the floor

James Babbs

Heavy On My Mind

dreams start streaming in
like the crack in the basement wall
where the rain rushed in
flooding across the floors
dreams pouring in
too fast for
the darkness to catch them all
they rise up and
spill over the edge
falling between the spaces and
I watch the faces floating past and
all of them remind me of you
in the morning leaving
traces of emptiness
weighing heavy on my mind

James Babbs

Jack and Coffee and the Rain Coming Down

not a good day today with
the rain coming down and
driving over a hundred miles
before making it back home
sitting at the kitchen table
looking out the window and
the rain falling down
the coffee in front of me
bottle of jack daniels and
I keep pouring it in the coffee
tasting it to make sure
it's enough and
the rain against the window
changes the appearance of things
it's only the middle of the week
but I feel like I'm trapped
inside the darkness of a tunnel
one light shining near the end
too far for me to reach

Richard Wink

Again over and over

Ugly morning starts with the glare of the sun,
I'm half blind but the introduction of vision matters less
as half my head is consumed by a stampede of industry
the other is in steep decline
and the picket line is manned by the lazy and the foul.

Lets continue with indifference
the silent treatment of you talking
I distracted
then a response
five minutes after the event

Wait till five and I exit half a man
the other half probably is still a kid fishing for utopia in
nineteen ninety six.
The last year
has been a series of black horses
and mid morning cigarettes

D.B. Cox

Stories to tell

back
in the "world"
with stories to tell

about things
he's seen
brutal, frightening

sometimes beautiful
things in vivid
heartbreaking detail

but as silence
walks him down easy
hometown streets

the tales die
inside his heart —
irrelevant recollections

that once burned
blood-red
in the dark

gone
cold as the ghosts
who breathed them

& he begins
to comprehend
how these shapes

carved

into his soul
are only words

& understands
how truly alone
he is

D.B. Cox

Searching for the door

night steps on stage
without fanfare-
an overlaid, underpaid lady
lingers at the intersection
of 12th street & absolute zero

distant-
like nobody can touch her
a high-stepper
with voodoo hips
perfume rising like a prayer
from her once retail body
lately relegated
to working the wholesale
side of the street-

hard-time hustler
with a face
like a city map folded
too many times-
sad eyes filled
with junk-sick rivers
she faces another night
made of waiting-

swaying in place
staring back
over her shoulder
as if she's searching
for the door
she came in through

D.B. Cox

Friday night in the drunk tank

floating over the drunk tank hum
a voice
at the back of the holding cell
demands a phone call

warm blood
begins to move
back into my numb hands
from cuffs — too tight

tiny shards of glass
from a beer-bottle bar fight
embedded in my
blood-matted hair

crystal ringing
in my brain
like a beautiful
girl's name

left eye swollen shut
thirteen dollars
stashed in the soles
of my old dingos

not enough for bail —
another friday night
in the city jail
for trying to make something

out of the emptiness
that crawls along
this boulevard
of half-remembered things

D.B. Cox

The ward

sometimes at night,
after the last light
has been doused,
& the holy meds

have rendered me
oblivious to the pain,
& night-smells
of the ward,

I can feel
the void
that stretches
out from my body
in every direction —

360 degrees
of seclusion,
dead as a disconnected
phone.

Sometimes,
I reach blindly into
that coal-black
absence,
hoping

my fingers
will brush
against
something
I can hold onto.

Maybe
a wayward angel,
who might
allow a little
unaccustomed mercy,

& lift me
above
these broken places;
back to the days
& faces,
I hadn't even known
I'd loved.

D.B. Cox

Dust-off

clean-collar commuters
peer from the cover
of stylish shades
taking secret comfort
in a pathetic apparition
wrapped
in an army overcoat
face down
in a pool of piss
baptized
purified
crucified
in the mute humility
of his own guilt
while inside crusty
rust-filled ears
distant city traffic
hums like a "huey" —
spectral medevac
searching for a soul
lost forty years ago
somewhere along
the mekong river

Robert Plath

One for Li Po

It's 9:00 A.M.
early May
I light a cigar
& walk out onto
the old stone patio
it rained all night
the forsythia are more
green than yellow
cherry blossom petals
stick to my shoes
my cigar smoke
drifts downward
toward the old covered
swimming pool then
vanishes above
brown leaves floating
in rainwater on top
of the sagging cover
the skin around my neck
is a little looser this year
I tap my ash in a puddle
in a while I'll pick up
a few bottles
cover the windows
with wool blankets
and turn out the lights
and dream away
in my womb of wine

Cynthia Ruth Lewis

Diluted

Blinded in the supermarket, walking dumbly through
the aisles, packing my cart high with sustenance;
steaks, breads, cakes, hoping to put some flesh
back on your whittled frame, hoping your sudden
plunge in weight is nothing serious, not the unspoken
"C," certainly, hoping the tests come back negative,
praying your three-times-a-day loose bowels are
due to some strange kind of flu, thinking I can
entice your appetite again with all this food as I
pile the cart higher and higher, until it is spilling
over with hope, adding melons to the mess,
fingers tightening around their wholeness, the
sweet perfection within as I watch children playing,
running from their mother's shouts, using cucumbers
as pistols, their innocent, ignorant bliss a knife in
my ribs, twisting ever so subtly. I advance numbly
to the check-out line, seeing people laugh amongst
themselves, bantering about recipes, grandchildren
and holiday gifts. I am a foreigner; amiss, not
understanding their words and grins, and I'm
fighting like hell not to break like glass, just shatter
at their feet when the clerk hands me the receipt
and says "Have a good Christmas," and I bite my
tongue to keep the tears from coming, biting down
hard until I can taste the blood, and only when I
can escape to the hooded density of my car do I
let it go, the tears running new and hot, diluting the
blood, the salt making it bearable, making it taste
just a little bit better.

Cynthia Ruth Lewis

Last words

Signing the papers,
finalizing my father's cremation,
they asked me if there was anything
I wanted to go along with him:
keepsakes, jewelry, anything?

All I could think of were words;
things I always wanted to say to him
that he never would have heard

I put it all in a letter to be burned,
and drove the next day in 100 degree heat
to avenge his death; unsaid words creased
neatly in my shirt pocket,
a monument to silence

The mortuary seemed a lifetime away,
further now than yesterday.
Perhaps it was only the heat,
the temperature stretching the asphalt
and stinging my eyes with sweat, the
thin paper now dampened at my breast,
words blurred beyond significance
and sense

Overhead, a few clouds push in,
distorting the atmosphere, the day,
casting everything in shades of
funereal gray...

even the sky loses its edge

Cynthia Ruth Lewis

Apathy

Just another day.
I rise, purposely overlooking your empty
side of the bed, dress, and go outside to
get some air, when I notice the bright
morning sun glinting off shards of glass
from the neighbor's newly-broken out window

I walk closer to investigate: screen's torn
off and flung to the side of the vacant
house, window-glass gaping wide—
wasn't sure if anyone might still be inside

Thought maybe I should call the neighbors
to let them know,
but, then again, the world unfortunately
being what it is, maybe I didn't see anything—
maybe it's not even broken

I go back inside, leaving the front door and
curtains wide, pass the unpaid bills on the
kitchen counter and sit down, light a cigarette,
and start to think, wondering exactly at what
particular point in my life it was that I
stopped giving a shit

Cynthia Ruth Lewis

Going by feel

I'm not sure exactly what was
going through my mind at the time;
all I knew was my fist twisting the
key in the ignition as I sped away
from you, wheels spitting gravel
and dust into the bruised eye of dawn,
not knowing where I was going, knowing
only that I was free, with the sting
of your five fingers still fresh on
my cheek, finally igniting the fire
under my ass that I had pissed into
forgiveness too many times, your stale
echo now fading in my ear that nobody
would want trash like me, anyhow, but
you sure clung like lint at any hint of
my leaving, and it felt good, damn good
to press that pedal all the way to the
fucking floor and scream away from you
with the windows down and the cold winter
air blowing my hair in my eyes, barely
able to see the road but going by feel,
knowing it was wide open and endless,
with the reliable hum of the engine to
guide me and some worn, familiar cracklings
on the old car radio to take me back to a
time when the sky was blue forever and I
never even knew your name

Lyn Lifshin

Like some lies we tell ourselves

the story of my father
on the phone, invited to
my wedding, bloomed then
settled into the landscape.
He's your father boy
friends would say, don't
you feel something? He
showed your poems to
Frost. The image of my
father in a chair listening
to the Dow Jones, saying
nothing hangs in the air
but yesterday I found
that letter I wrote
after my husband to be
called and my father
blurted: I don't care
about her. I don't want
to come to your wedding,
hear about it, be involved.
And I don't want to pay.
It flares open, a yucca
plant that takes 100 years
to bloom, floods the night
with a peculiar scent and
I think how I've hated
cheap men, one sign and
I'm running. I think how,
dead so long, even today
my father takes up too
much space

Lyn Lifshin

The other fathers

would be coming back
from some war, sending
back stuffed birds or
a handkerchief in navy
blue with Love painted
on it. Some sent telegrams
for birthdays, the pasted
letters like jewels. The
magazines for children
were full of fathers who
were doing what had
to be done, were serving,
were brave. Someone
said there'd be confetti
in the streets and maybe
no school, that soon we'd
have bananas. My father
sat in the grey chair,
war after war, hardly
said a word at dinner. I
wished he had gone away
with the others so maybe
he would be coming
back to us

Lyn Lifshin

My father's wallet

maybe he abandoned it long before he abandoned us.
He lived in the same house, moving past us in the hall,
sat, without a word at the chrome kitchen table until
my mother moved out first, took a spring cottage at the
lake where my cat got treed and firemen came to the
rescue.
After that, Othello was not let off the porch. By summer,
we were back in our own apartment and my father took
rooms at a house in town, hitched up and down rt 7
after
my mother took his key to the Pontiac. To break the
gloom, I thought I would marry and invited him to
come.
"I don't want to be involved or pay," he hissed on the
phone, the last words he'd say to me except once, when
I ran into him in the Post Office when he whispered,
"Don't do anything you don't want." He hadn't even
wanted to send my sister or me to college, just cared
about the stocks, wanted them to be a memorial to him,
never go to his wife or daughters but invest themselves
until the world collapsed like a space ship lost in orbit,
circling endlessly with no way to escape. This wallet
must have been as much a time capsule of what he
could walk away from as easily as his heart did from us,
with its birth certificate listing a date I never knew and
the town of Vilna in the county of Vilnius, a page that
looked like an old confederate bill, a few pennies from
the 20's, as useless to him as I guess we were

Lyn Lifshin

September 23, 1996

A red tide in Texas, a
red tide between my
sister and I. This day
of forgiveness, we
don't talk, haven't.
I wonder if she's
beginning another
diet with a fast. Or
maybe she's gotten
rid of her fat the way
she shed most of her
family, wonder if she
has dyed her hair, is
rigging up telescopes,
saving refugees or
walling herself in with
acres of Holocaust
books, cages to lock
her turtles in. Towels
over the window. No
one is sure where the
poison in the tide
comes from, what to
do with it, how long
it will ruin things

Lyn Lifshin

Almost the way she stood in the bathroom with the door locked at two

tearing my mother up,
making my father climb
to the roof next door,
go thru the motions
of unlocking the door.
He begged and pleaded,
cajoled, coddled, waited.
Somehow they opened
that door as they couldn't
others deeper inside her
past the blonde beauty
hair, blue eyes that made
me sure she was adopted.
She locked doors in her
head, ran with horses,
men who wouldn't or
would leave their wives,
lashed out, bruising,
bruised, suing leaves off
the tree, suing the sun
for daring to enter. She
blocked windows, caged
cats, caged herself
behind pounds that hide
her once perfect body.
She puts up bars, double
locks her nightmares,
flings her fists like an
infant cutting the air into
shreds fast as blades of
a fan you can't tell are
spinning in circles unless

you get too near

Lafayette Wattles

Death Comes In Smallness

I remember the day recess stopped being
the last preservation of fun. We had
quit playing four-square in the sun
to watch a hawk take something dark
from the field, and the teacher
said it was a mouse, only it was more.
For, until that moment, life had been
this huge thing we were all part of,
but none of us thought about
how small it becomes once it's given a body
or that death comes in smallness, too.
And, as if some greater force needed
to make this clear, sirens called us, then,
to the front of the school, where we found
two men in white loading the ambulance.
Being slaves to the spectacle of the unknown,
we cheered, as they drove away,
unaware that my sister was the mystery,
that she had swollen shut—her eyes, mouth,
throat—from a couldn't even see it
hint of cinnamon, and, to this day, when I see
a hawk circling the sky, searching, searching,
as I have all these years, I pull
to the side of the road, and say goodbye.

Lafayette Wattles

Something More

Hot summer nights
we'd watch the widow next door
from the top floor of the maple —
the one dad lopped one afternoon
while we were lost at school —
and you'd pretend to be her lover,
before we knew anything about loving
anyone but our-own-teen-selves,
and you'd put on that thick French
accent with your lips plumped out
as if she wore some special magnetic suit
beneath her nakedness
polarized just for your kisses,
and you'd say, *Oui, oui, mon cheri,*
I would love to love you and only you,
and, as if she could hear you,
she'd dance like a feather
on a breath of air, light, soft,
window opened wide,
until the night we caught dad
standing near the trunk whispering
words he was supposed to save
for mom, and the widow
must have heard or seen him,
there, below us, for she clutched
her drapes, gasped, then saw me, you,
two featherless birds gawking
with our beaks flung wide,
our hunger for her replaced by fear,
and dad said, *Oh, Shit!* and ducked
behind the tree until he realized
she had eyes for us, and I was ready
to jump, then, from the limbs,

the way you had done from our youth,
but you smiled at me and mouthed,
She's seen us and is still there,
just as dad grabbed your foot
like a loose branch, shook you free,
then me, but he didn't say anything,
what could he say,
so he just dragged us by our ears
to the house, and you didn't see
how I took the pain, how I twisted
back, as the drapes drew closed,
how the widow seemed to linger,
there, and sigh, I was sure of it,
as I caught one last glorious hint
of thigh, of hip, of breast
and thought, just then, that
maybe we weren't the only ones
collecting something more than memories
those hot summer nights.

Michele Leavitt

Seven to Life

Why did I stay? His hands, like carved white pine,
touched my swollen face, and it was better

than no touch at all. It was never good.
The day we met, I chased a starling from my window

to the open air, it left small black feathers
pasted on the frame. We had both read Dostoevsky,

both suffered beatings from those that we adored,
and didn't we believe that suffering purifies

the soul? North country winters kill all that's weak
and inessential --- split limbs of tamaracks, warblers

that put off leaving until the first big snow.
I don't believe it now, but then, suffering

was the only door out of the dinginess of wanting,
out of a life as empty as a hollowed-out t.v.

And today, if I were to open that door, he'd be there,
the one face that never fades.

The one face I never want to see again.
I meant to leave him, asleep in a wooden room,

I was wearing bad shoes, too skimpy for the walk
across the frozen Kennebec to the next town. I stayed

with friends, rolled in a red sleeping bag
on a linoleum floor, but I was bad luck, no fun,

always in the way. He tracked me down, and cried.
I meant to leave.

*　*　*

Rail tracks run along the river, the river-road,
the throat, the vein, all passageways that must have

destinations. I meant to travel, got hung up
on the whistle stops along the way. Fields

of daffodils, too golden to bear, their heads nodding
as mine did above a red kitchen table,

and a glassine bag, holding one more dose,
labeled "7 - 2 -Life." A dealer's idea of poetry.

A prison term. A destiny. Till death do us part.
Glassine, so smooth, sounding like a stream

I could slip away on. I meant to leave him dead
in that apartment, with all the bills,

the rented furniture, the borrowed Navy blanket
covering our stained bed, stenciled "U. S.,"

us, a bad joke. I did get out. I poured
oblivion down all my body's rivers.

I forgot how to stay.

*　*　*

Still, my guts hold an appetite for drama,
for a man who'll lift me by my shoulders,

kiss my breasts one moment, slam me

up against a wall the next, wailing he knows

another man has touched me, then get on his knees
to beg forgiveness. I've carried

this craving from town to town, this lust
for pain and touch to make my life feel real,

this habit harder to kick than the dope.
It's time to clean up my hand. I keep going out,

climbing the trail that crawls up
the mountainside from my cabin. Sometimes,

an eagle and a flock of ravens circle the peak,
fighting their little wars. They swoop and scream

and tear at one another. Like what I remember
lovers to be. I always want to leave,

but if the eagle's white tail is backlit
by the sun, there's eerie grace in their battling

in the lonely air: they are the only life, relief
from the emptiness of heaven,

so I stay. They make prey of each other,
dripping their blood and fluff down the ridge fissures,

where it mixes with the springmelt
that rushes now, too, toward riverbeds

etched like veins in the granite
of the valley floor. I meant to leave it all,

stranded high up on the bank, in fragments
left for dead, forgetting.

Again over and over

Greg Scharf

One For The Metaphysicians, Or...

The guy who lives
in the dilapidated
2 bedroom house
across the alley
whistles a tune spiritedly
after he steps out
of his beat-up Honda,
wearing his ubiquitous
gray work shirt
with the rectangular patch
bearing his name
("Norman")
in red cursive.

He whistles like a man
who just hit the lottery,
or got his dick sucked
by a thick lipped super model,
or been told by his doctor
the lump is benign,
or discovered that God really does exist
and has agreed to save him.

But he whistles like this everyday,
which renders those explanations
even more absurd
than they already are.

What could it be?

I've seen his wife waddling after their ill-mannered dog,
I've heard his kid wailing for attention,
I breathe the same polluted air he breathes,

I eat the same greasy, genetically modified food,
I touch myself during moments of loneliness
as I'm sure he does too.

So what is it
that makes him whistle
like that?

If the metaphysicians ever get a hold of him
they might discover
what they've been looking for all along...

or maybe this is one for the head shrinks.

Greg Scharf

I love you in other words

Marie says,
"Let me go,"
as she fills her cupped hands
with tears
and I blow smoke
at the noon heat hanging
like Satan lynched
outside her second story window.

Last week she broke down
like an old dodge bought on 6th street
for a C-note,
so the doctor prescribed Xanax
and the writing of therapeutic screeds
about me in her bedside
journal.

She wants a man she can introduce
to her friends
A man who'll go to office parties
and mingle and talk sports
with her successful, socially well-adjusted
colleagues
Someone who'll have something normal
to say when the nice lady
from Human Resources asks,
"So what is it you do?"
Something more appropriate than:
"Eat, drink, shit and fuck."

So it's up to me
to do the right thing
and "let her go"
No more horny midnight phone calls

No more lies about what I did the night before
No more drunken speeches about life and death
No more racing my twisted soul
down her straight and narrow heart

She often asks if I love her
and I guess
if I can do this then
I do.

Greg Scharf

I wanted to write something nice about love but ended up writing this instead

I guess there was something
more important
than a few more kisses,
something more
that another
redundant Friday night
had to offer
to let IT
slip away
like a dead fish
through fingers stained
in scaly iridescence,
which is now all
either of us has left
of the experience.

I know there are
plenty more mutated fish
in this polluted sea
and I've seen
your bright barbed hooks
and don't doubt
you'll catch your limit.

Good
luck.

But as for me
I'm gonna hold my breath
beneath the surface
secure inside
my steel

shark-proof cage
where neither fish
nor fisherwoman
can catch me,

and I'm gonna hold out
for a mermaid
worth parting
with these steel bars…

I guess I'm still not above
believing in myths.
But love?
That one
is just a little
too fantastic
to swallow
and even if I did
swallow it
I'd probably just
end up
choking
on the bones
anyway.

Keith Niles

It's just me, mid-madness

The fact that I'm a suddenly middle aged man with lava lamps in the living room of his one bedroom apartment, up all night compiling cds and slapping cheese tacos onto the dingy burners of his stove, traipsing blindly through young girl minefields, breaking down and beating off and thrashing back wildly against the brutal viccisitudes of luck, fuck, this fact, these facts are not lost upon me, but it feels true, what can I say, what can I do?

The fact that I slack back and take whacks at the pot pipe at this point in my life then dash out into the night to rage through drunken storms along rank strangers staggering home later to again engage the notebook page is not strange to me if not altogether sage, believe me, I know, trust me, I see....

I have earned all my newfound freedom, have surfaced from years of suspended claymation, seen the truth, I've grown out of personas of shyness and competence and failure, personas that never quite fit me, domesticity and work and normalcy, I've sprouted again, grown a soul, and donned the wingtips of youth.

So if you spot me through the blind late Thursday night bathed in blue light, high, lava roiling, bobblehead triangulated between oversized speakers, leafing through lyrics and dreaming of fruition, wet Modello in off hand, right leg humping the couch as the groove insists itself upon the vicinity, if you see me filling notebooks black with shallow adolescent lacks of this and lacks of that, girls and drunk-ons and friendless sads, fighting back against the forces real or imagined that are charring me black, if you see me trying too hard to star in this whatever play in which I've weaseled a bit part, know this, know that, know that I've worked hard to be free, that I've earned every last bit of innocence you might see and everything else is just me--it's just me!

Keith Niles

The lows of Vegas

How to describe the lows of Vegas, some of the lowest lows, a tiredness that goes deep into your soul, the lonely vacuity of your room, the dryness of your bunghole, as you lie there hating the smell of yourself, the restlessness of your lowest desires keeping you awake, particularly odd and scary if you're up seventeen, eighteen hundred bucks and you don't know what the fuck to do with yerself but carefully spit fifty dollar drabs of it away here and there, knowing you should be thrilled with your fortunes, but knowing too that money sickness is all over you and the dry heat, drunkenness, lack of sleep and sudden seeming absence of a soul have carved out hollows of your insides…

Karl Koweski

They call me Captain Gringo

Charles the incompetent
third shift maintenance man
brought the books to work
in two Reebok shoe boxes

the name of the author
escapes me – an obvious
pseudonym given the books
pornographic nature

the twenty nine volumes
were gathered under the
RENEGADE imprint and
chronicled the turn of
the century adventures
of Captain Gringo and
his lusty French sidekick,
Gustave, who during the
course of their south of
the border campaigns
fucked a vast array of
senoritas, sheep,
paraplegics, prairie dogs,
and a guy named Lou

not to be outdone
Captain Gringo with his
nine inch tool also
fucked everything that
walked or crawled or
galloped and what he
didn't fuck he usually
killed with his twin

gatlin guns and often he'd
be called upon to kill
what three pages earlier
he had thoroughly fucked

Charles swore up and
down these books were
classic literature and
before long we were
agreeing with him

men who hadn't picked up
anything meatier than the
Sunday Times devoured the
books at a three a week clip

I found the books to be
hackneyed and obvious
poorly written throughout
but I read them anyway
imagining myself tearing
through the Mexican low
lands, fucking the
General's twin daughters,
his wife, their housekeeper,
and the bushy tailed
Pomeranian before going to
town and rampaging through
the populace with my big
dick and blazing guns of fury

and when I glanced about
I noticed my co-workers
also walking with a bit
of a swagger looking for
men to challenge, women
to ravage and stray dogs

to cornhole, and finding
none, returning to their
machines and the dog-eared
paperbacks hidden beneath
their work instructions

twelve Captain Gringos
and not a Gustave among us

Karl Koweski

Art and Commerce

I learned the correlation
between the two
at the age of six
when, having crayoned
through an entire
coloring book, I showed
the results to my father
for his artistic critique

a day later he gave me
a dollar and said
he sold the coloring book
to a lady at work

even so young, my dad's
words struck me
as implausible

why would anyone want
to buy a coloring
book that's all
ready been colored?

my dad furrowed his
brow and said something
about the woman's son
having been born with
flippers for arms
unable to color his
own coloring books

the explanation was
good enough for me

I rifled through my room
gathering all my old
coloring books and
during a hand cramping
crayola marathon
managed to fill every
blank page therein

I presented the
eight books to my
dad the next night
estimating there was
enough capital represented
in that pile for
at least three G.I. Joes

he returned the next day
empty-handed
citing market saturation
and an increase
of suppliers versus
a decrease in customers

but I figured he just
took the money he made
off my toil and spent
the cash on cheap whiskey

M.K. Chavez

Americana

The dogs beg for Prozac
but we tell them to suck it up,
get straight, do their duty.
It's dog eat dog.
The TV's are buzzing
we watch the world
on a 19 inch screen,
we weep for reality
weight loss, and game show survivors.
Memory is televised
the ocean, the sky and the stars
are pre-programmed.
There's no escaping the noise
the relentless guttural roar of cars.
Jaguars, Rams, Eagles, Mustangs,
Vipers and Hybrids; the nature of American life.
Life is gray. Everything is cold, concrete, cash
units and measurements of what we're worth.
It's another night, loneliness
is screaming its scheduled scream.
Wheels spin on tracks that take us
back and forth to places were we'd rather not
be. We're too tired to move. We hold on
for the intermission, the station break,
the revision of history. We watch the news,
immobilized and hypnotized. We watch
for the next disaster
for the next time we can feel
for the next time we can cry
We mourn predictably.

Close your eyes.
Hold a perfect pose.

Let the buzz of the television
fill the empty space.
This is the way
they want you to be.
Still
as quiet as a statue
the image of All-American liberty.

Joseph Veronneau

Roadside

Up by the bridge
mangy men stand bow-legged,
hands deep into their
jean pockets.
The street is pot-holed,
cars cruise thru and nearly lose
their front bumpers,
the aroma of glazed tar
spanning the site.

Twenty of them sit by
the side of the road idle;
one talks on a cell phone
as cables are being planted
underground
or so I am told.

They will not finish there
for some time to come,
the paycheck is good
and beats unemployment.
So the cars will continue
their illegal u-turns
and people will continue
to raise their arms to the air
as if God will better direct this traffic
right after his lunch break.

Joseph Veronneau

Unspoken

Deep within the barracks
the poems written sat
like suicide letters;
blown walls formed smoky havens
as all of their unknown contents
sifted up in smoke,
unspoken, ungiven
not a soul touched
by them. They slept
with the bodies of men
where windows no longer counted
and there was no need for explanation.

Joseph Veronneau

At the Dinner Table

At the checker table-clothed table
my grandparents called each other lying
bastards, old witch, and clueless,
if not for my uncle having been
excluded from conversation
due to drunkeness,
my other uncle too busy talking about
his latest pick-up line
and the latest fox he had met
at the local pub,
had it not been that
the dog was readily available
to chow down
whatever unidentifiable food it was
that I tossed under the table,
or that we were all being warped
by the microwave which sat
no more than a foot behind all of us
and that we were all poisoned from its deathrays,
had these not been truths
I would have asked to have been excused
much earlier.

Nathan A. Baker

Fathers and Sons

Down by the old Springfield mill
Where waste water churned spume
And local boys in summertime swam
Bare-ass in the cold brown waters

The two of us would walk, silence
Caressing like an ineffective balm,
Unable to sooth the roughness
Or lessen the guilt fed friction

That chaffed the space between us.
Ideally there is a way things should be
But reality gives you life… things
The way they are… no questions.

Some lessons are learned too late.
I should have left my rags,
Soiled with childhood's memories,
Beside that polluted creek

And jumped in naked maybe then
He too would have found his way.

Nathan A. Baker

An Urn of Ashes

All she had left was memories
And an old clock, its walnut frame
Smooth like time in its passing,
Worn where edges once were crisp

He left her when she was just a baby,
Nearly a hatchling, still she longed
For her daddy just as any girl would
And at age of sagacity found him

In a one-night pit stop and market
Openly catering to appetites rare.
Flesh being flesh and the human need
Being strong as it is, she danced

Every dance known before she ever
Danced her first one with me.
Tripping the full circle a time or two
All the freaking way around

Without ever stopping or taking
The time to come up for air, but
His presence in her life would not
Have stopped her decline into the pit

Her journey was long ago destined
Set upon by the course of the wind

Mather Schneider

Bananas

After crossing the border at Nogales
we can breathe again.
Driving home through Arizona
her Mexican divorce papers in the glove
she holds tight to me and to the promise
of making money
like two porpoise-dreams pulling her
through a river of uselessness.

She's small and dark and lovely
and kind, and we can hardly speak to each other
but it doesn't matter.

So what if love
is a lie
where we agree to meet?

She feeds me pieces of banana with her little
terra cotta fingers
and laces the air with a silver-toothed smile
and tosses the greasy yellow peel
out onto the hardpan shoulder of the highway
while I drive under the raw Sonoran sun
and butcher my Spanish to tell her
what I think is important in life,
which doesn't take long:
letting go of shame.

We have agreed, we have
decided, we have been swept away
while letting ourselves,
and we have, somehow, slipped
through.

Mather Schneider

Scooter

She's thirty six and ugly as a gargoyle
every bad gene imaginable
funneled into her
like green beer into the mouth
of a slut
and here she is in my cab
with her Tom Selleck mustache
and her wine barrel figure
and her arthritis and excuses
and her peroxide blond hair frizzy
as death by chair
and her bound-sausage feet and Micheline Man legs
and two-ham ass
and blood-blossoms of acne
mixed with cheap make-up like
strawberry icing on her foul cake face.
She rolls the window up
and lights a smoke.
She hasn't had a job in fifteen years
just lets other people take care of her
like me giving her a free ride home from the doctor
because she hurt her foot
walking to the bathroom.
All the way to her government-subsidized house she bitches
because nobody will give her
a free scooter...
And when I get close to her house
I miss her street accidently
(I've never been there before)
and I have to stop and turn around
she snickers and snorts
like I'm the biggest

idiot loser ever
to limp
across the piss-poor earth.

John Grochalski

One of the best

he was born to a narcissistic nag
and a car salesmen
in new orleans
and maybe the madness was already
setting in then
but he managed to make good
with a college degree
and a master's degree
and a few teaching gigs
in new york city and louisiana
until he gave it up
to hang with musicians in
the french quarter
selling tamales from a cart
and working in a clothing factory
all while the madness kept bubbling
from below
and he started pounding away
on a machine at night
writing beautiful insanity
a prose that "isn't really about anything,"
as the big book houses
kept telling him in rejections
but he knew he had it
he knew he had the genius and words down
the way they should be
but he couldn't quite make it happen
he got hooked on the drink
he got hooked on his domineering mother
and some people said that maybe
he was a fag because the writing
and the booze and his mother
left him no time for a piece of ass.

then one day he blew a gasket
and just disappeared
he took a car and barreled it to the west coast
and then all the way back to georgia
to have a drink with the ghost of flannery o'connor
before driving off to biloxi
to put a garden hose full of car exhaust down
deep into his gut
leaving the world less than what it was before
and the rest of us silly word slingers failing
just to catch a whiff of his lunatic soul

John Grochalski

Lessons from a master

this sandy beach
those girls in small brown bikinis
playing volleyball near
the surf
this seaside bar
full of pictures from the 19th century
and over-priced beer.
we've been sitting here
for two hours
sucking at bud lights
and smelling the fried clams
while the elf sitting next to us
talks to himself
and nurses a draft
keeps getting up to play
the same five songs on the jukebox
aretha franklin's "freeway"
sinatra
louis prima
petula clark
the bird is the word, man.
he had everyone dancing at first
moving their heads
lightly tapping their bottles
against the bar
he was the musical madman of the joint
playing everything we all wanted
to hear.
people smiled
and winked at him
but come the third round
of the same songs
the place started to thin out

sick of aretha
and sinatra and all of the rest
but the elf just sat there taking in the music
singing as loud
as he could
as seat after seat cleared
he just sat there laughing
this four-foot tall genius
an unsung master
the best i'd ever seen
at clearing out a room.

John Grochalski

Success

you always wanted to do
the big thing
be the guy on stage
the one who has all eyes on him
when he walks into a room
a man, who when he speaks,
you can hear a pin drop otherwise.

but you know it'll never be that way
all those thoughts are just hyperbole
something to keep you warm
when there's no one around
and the world just keeps getting colder
and everyone's stories are always
just a touch better than your own

the adoring crowd
the fawning girls in the sun
with the light casting on their faces
on their sparse, lanuginous hairs
waiting for you
the dream friends in dream cars
the big nights of victory
on neon drenched streets
full of endless hours

sometimes you're so noir, it hurts

the thing is you never had
a gauge for what success really was
surrounded by all the failures of the hoi polloi
success was what you saw on television
or what existed in your head

on those dark, december evenings
along the paper route
in those juvenile bouts of insomnia
dreaming the perfect future
with the walkman piercing the night

you never realized that it could
be right here in this cluttered room
surrounded by four asylum walls on a hot street
scotch dizzy in a wine-soaked t-shirt
with no end to the drought
where the stained windows give everything
and elegant tint
and no one even knows that you're alive.

Duncan Fankboner

In the middle of the last century

dusty run down windows
walls strung along just for fun
rocks up the hill
just the right size for throwing
old factory town
dirt roads in and out
you'd think
there'd be somewhere to go
nothing like that
what we had
a baseball field
a vacant lot
weeds and baseball gloves
splayed swollen fingers
a ball with
some torn leather around it
all that
and the spirit of things
bigger wider
than anything we could understand
playing till the light was down
till a cold wind blew us home
to rented houses calls
from back porches
hunger just another spirit
holding us together
54' the year
school and the excitement
of girls who wanted to kiss
and school books
filled with lies and mystery

Duncan Fankboner

Not the buddha

Johnny Utah
sat still on the head
waiting for the birth
of one long warm turd
later that day
after the sun rose
he felt down and lay low
on his bed with the shades
drawn
in the night a storm
filled the sky
and lightening shone
and thunder saw it
and felt a little envious
even though he didn't know
the lightening had listened
for his moan
Johnny left home that night
and rode on a train deep
into the east passing many
atomic particles of air
he would not come back
nor were there any memories
of the place he had left
not of home
or the city
not of anything
not even
you

J.J. Campbell

The bullets of ignorance

struggling with the
demons on a rainy
monday morning
again
bracing myself for
yet another week
of dodging the
bullets of ignorance
and god knows
whatever else happens
to get under my weary
sensitive skin
for i know there will
be some poor soul
that will ask me why
am i overweight,
unemployed and jaded
here in the 21st century
and i'll laugh and tell
this person that i have
no desire to live any
longer than i absolutely
have to
i'll leave that person
dumbfounded and
stewing in their
confusion
and it's that confusion
that leads me to believe
i'm the one
on the right
path

J.J. Campbell

A war of attrition

caught here in the trappings
of the next big music act
from sweden
wondering which suicide is this

and how i always wanted my
death to be romantic, epic,
truly what everyone would call
"a moment"

but i've painfully learned over
the years that this life
is a war of attrition
and nothing beautiful comes from war
no matter how blind my
mind's eye truly is

misery keeps me company anymore
at a mere dollar a glass

i must have caught the bartender
in a mood or she can
smell the desperation as plainly
as i wear it

we'll close this joint down tonight

the after hours though, will be
in the hands of a god that has
clearly given up on me
or it's another case of the joke
being something
over my head completely

either is possible
but now is not the time

there are glasses that
need to be refilled

Cortney Davis

Hooked up

Drunk, partying, she
and the man just *hooked up*
she tells me, the college student, the nervous
can't-sit-still woman,
dark-haired, laughing, pierced tongue,
pierced navel, colored threads
braided into bracelets around her wrist,
barely making it through finals,
graduating next spring then
maybe a Master's, but for today,
she says, the problem is fear,
What if I caught something, this worry
hooked into her and now
she slides down, eager but not eager
for me to do cultures, blood tests,
to tell her everything is fine.
Oh how often I've seen this,
this fear twisted in as if there might be
a tangle inside, shiny, metallic,
like wire, and how each time
I have to pull it out,
strand by strand,
trying not to weep over this
one more woman hooked up,
these barbs deep into flesh,
and how they can only be extracted
with moans and cries, each one
ripping through until
there is no more innocence,
only this woman and me,
helpless to do anything
but go on pulling the hooks from her,
stuffing them into the garbage,

telling her how sweet they must have seemed
that night, how she must learn to recognize them
before they gain entrance; how strong
she must be now, how resolute.

Cortney Davis

First Night at the Cheap Hotel

Tonight, the moon is almost full, its glow filtered
through my window's small, square screen.
Down the hall, a man coughs and coughs.
There are women's voices too, tinny, high,
like a sound from childhood,
the fluted, aluminum milk bottle caps
Mother pierced and jangled on a string.
In my room, the middle note of the air conditioner
and something caught inside the fan, rattling—no,
crackling—
like the crackling of air under skin, crepitus.
Being here is like being sick in a hospital ward
without the lovely, muffling glove of illness.
In hospital, I would be drowsy, drugged into a calm
that accepts the metal door's clang,
the heavy footfall right outside my door.
All these would be proof of life,
and there would be a nurse too, who would
hold my wrist, counting and nodding,
only a silhouette in the dark.
As my mother did, she'd hold her finger to her lips,
saying shhh, shhh, and, like a child,
feverish, safe,
I would close my eyes, and sleep.

Bios

James Babbs
James Babbs' recent poems have appeared in his dreams and in *Barbaric Yawp, Hazmat Review, Poetry East, Rural Messengers Press,* and *Snow Monkey.*

Nathan A. Baker
Nathan is a carpenter/poet living in the mountains of Tennessee. His poetry has appeared in *Red River Review, Tamafyhr Mountain Poetry, Lily, Underground Window, Zafusy,* and *Blue House.*

J.J. Campbell
J.J. Campbell (b. 1976) lives, writes but mostly dies a little each day in Brookville, Ohio. He's been widely published over the years, most notably in *Zygote in My Coffee, Nerve Cowboy, Chiron Review, Thunder Sandwich,* and *Babel Magazine.*

Carol Carpenter
Carol Carpenter's poems and stories have appeared in numerous online and print publications, including *Margie, Snake Nation Review, Birmingham Arts Journal, Georgetown Review, Caveat Lector, Orbis, Arabesques Review,* and various anthologies, the most recent are *Not What I Expected* (Paycock Press, 2007) and *A Walk Through My Garden* (Outrider Press, 2007). Her work has been exhibited by art galleries and produced as podcasts (Connecticut Review and Bound Off). She received the Richard Eberhart Prize for Poetry, the Jean Siegel Pearson Poetry Award, Artists Among Us Award and others. Formerly a college writing instructor, journalist and trainer, she now writes full time in Livonia, Michigan.

M.K. Chavez
Bay Area Poet M.K. Chavez writes about strippers, the beauty that can be found in ugliness, the mystery of feeling bad about feeling good, little birds, big consequences. Her work has been anthologized and is published online and in print. *Virgin Eyes*, a chapbook of poetry is being published by Zeitgeist Press. Most recent and upcoming publications include *Poesy, Poems-for-All, Snow Monkey*, and *Instant Pussy*.

D.B. Cox
D.B. Cox can be found in the early-morning hours, bent over a Fender Stratocaster, in roadhouses and juke joints throughout the south. He describes his playing style as "a look at life through drunken, godless eyes." To quiet his tortured soul, he writes. Two of his short stories, "Road Like A River" and "Before Tomorrow" have been nominated for Pushcart Prizes. He has published four books of poetry. His first chapbook is entitled *Passing For Blue*, and is available from Rank Stranger Press. Two other chapbooks, *Lowdown* and *Ordinary Sorrows*, are available from Pudding House Publications. His latest collection called *Empty Frame* can be picked up on-line at Main Street Rag Publishing.

Dennis Cruz
Born in San Jose, Costa Rica, Dennis Cruz migrated to Los Angeles with his mother when he was only six months old. Growing up all over L. A., he attended thirteen public schools within the Los Angeles Unified School District. He is a self-taught poet who derives his inspiration from having survived extraordinary circumstances as a child. He has been writing steadily for twenty years, and has performed at various L.A. venues, including Beyond Baroque and the World Stage, and has also appeared on public radio stations KXLU

and KPFK. *The Beast Is We* is the latest of his eight chapbooks of prose and poetry.

Ron D'Alena
Ron D'Alena's work has recently appeared or is forthcoming in *A cappella Zoo, Word Riot, Cause & Effect Magazine, Johnny America, Goldfish Press, 94 Creations, Falling Star Magazine, Persephonous Blue,* and *Slipstream.*

Cortney Davis
Cortney Davis is a nurse practitioner at a women's health clinic in Danbury, Conn. As a writer, Davis has garnered an NEA Poetry Fellowship and two poetry grants from the Connecticut Commission on the Arts. Her latest poetry collection is *Leopold's Maneuvers*. Most recently, her essay was showcased on NPR.

John Dorsey
John Dorsey currently resides in Toledo, OH. He is the author of *Harvey Keitel, Harvey Keitel, Harvey Keitel* with S.A. Griffin and Scott Wannberg (Butchershop Press/Rose of Sharon Press/Temple of Man, 2005) and *Moshing With The Cosmos* with Iris Berry (Magenta Press, 2005).

R.C. Edrington
R.C. Edrington has been a scourge on the small press for years. You can find his scribbles in countless journals, ezines, anthologies, and chapbooks. He currently writes, fights off the urge to become a full time hermit, and kicks empty cans thru the dope induced potholes in his memory...

S.A. Griffin
S.A. Griffin is the author of *Unborn Again* (Phony Lid), *A One Legged Man Standing Casually On Hollywood Blvd. Smoking A Cigarette* (1989, Shelf Life Press), *Heaven Is One Long Naked Dance* (1993, Rose of Sharon Press), *Twisted*

Cadillac: A Spoken Word Odyssey (with The Carma Bums, 1996, Sacred Beverage Press) and Co-Editor of *The Outlaw Bible of American Poetry* (1999, Thunder's Mouth Press).

John Grochalski
John Grochalski is a published writer whose poems have appeared in *Avenue, The Lilliput Review, The New Yinzer, The Blue Collar Review, The Deep Cleveland Junkmail Oracle, The ARTvoice, Modern Drunkard Magazine, The American Dissident, Words-Myth, My Favorite Bullet, The Main Street Rag, Thieves Jargon, Underground Voices, Why Vandalism, Eclectica, Zygote In My Coffee, Gloom Cupboard*, and forthcoming in the *Kennesaw Review, Octopus Beak Inc.,* and *Cherry Bleeds*. His short fiction has appeared in the *Pittsburgh Post-Gazette*, and in the forthcoming anthology *Living Room Handjob*. Grochalski's column The Lost Yinzer appears quarterly in *The New Yinzer* (www.newyinzer.com), and his book of poems *The Noose Doesn't Get Any Looser After You Punch Out* is forthcoming via Six Gallery Press.

Daryl Horton
Daryl Horton is a Marine, poet, boxer from South Carolina. Currently searching life and documenting experiences. Stay tuned for more.

Debbie Kirk
Debbie Kirk is a writer from Austin, Texas. She has been published in such places as *Open Wide, Warm Angel Whiskey, Babel, Fearless, Spent Meat,* and *Underground Voices*.

Karl Koweski
Karl Koweski is a thirty year old displaced Chicagoan now living on top of a mountain in Alabama. He's been published throughout the small press and internet and in such places as *Hustler Fantasies, Swank, Night Terrors*

and in anthologies like *It's All Good* from Manic D Press and *Trip the Light Fantastic*. He has a collection of stories, *Playthings*, out through Future Tense Press and several poetry chapbooks, most recently *Can't Kill A Man Born To Hang* published by Bottle of Smoke Press.

Michele Leavitt
Michele Leavitt is a former trial attorney who now teaches in The Writing Program at the University of North Florida. Her poems and essays have been published in a variety of journals and anthologies, including *Rattapallax, The NeoVictorian/Cochlea, Slant, Sojourner, The Humanist, Wind, The Ledge, Yellow Silk II: International Erotic Stories and Poems, Asheville Poetry Review, The Edge City Review,* and *THEMA*.

Cynthia Ruth Lewis
Cynthia Ruth Lewis has been writing on and off for the past twenty years. She can be found in *Cherry Bleeds, Underground Voices, Zygote in My Coffee,* and other venues. *Piss on Your Parade,* a collection of her work, can be obtained by emailing *bookas6670@yahoo.com*.

Lyn Lifshin
Just out from Lyn Lifshin: *The Licorice Daughter: My Year With Ruffian* and *Another Woman Who Looks Like Me*. She has over 120 published books & has edited 4 anthologies. Her last two Black Sparrow books *Cold Comfort* and *Before It's Light* won Paterson Review Awards. New also: *In Mirrors, an unfinished story, The daughter I don't have,* and *She was found treading water*. Her website: www.lynlifshin.com

John Macker
John Macker's most recent book is *Adventures In The Gun Trade*, (Las Vegas: Long Road/Temple of Man, 2004). Previous books include *The First Gangster* and *Burroughs*

At Santo Domingo. He lives in the foothills of the Sangre de Cristo Mountains in northern New Mexico.

Keith Niles
Keith Niles lives in Los Angeles. His collection, K*iss the bongwater* (knownothing press), is said to shatter the boundaries between humankind and the cat world.

Tony O'Neill
Tony O'Neill's autobiographical novel *Digging The Vein* was published in Feb 2006 by Contemporary Press, in the US and Canada. Wrecking Ball Press released a UK edition April 2007. *Seizure Wet Dreams*, a collection of short stories and poems was released in the UK on Social Disease, January 2006. A volume of poetry, *Songs From The Shooting Gallery*, was released on Burning Shore Press, Spring 2007. *Down And Out On Murder Mile*, his new novel, was released in October 2008 by Harper Perennial. He also is the co-author of *Hero Of The Underground*, the memoir of Jason Peter [2008, St Martins Press]. He lives in New York.

Robert Plath
Robert Plath has one book of published poems called *Ashtrays and Bulls* (2003 1st place winner of Nerve Cowboy's chapbook contest). He has published poems in *Barfing Dog Press, Big City Lit, Blowback, Chiron Review, Devil Blossoms, Evolution, Gnome, Long Island Quarterly, Lunatic Chameleon, Mad Swirl, Mannequin Envy, Nerve Cowboy, Pearl, Poetrybay, Polarity, Sho, Soul Fountain, Stickman Review, The Idiot,* and *Zygote in my Coffee*. He also has poems forthcoming in *Cerebral Catalyst, decomP, Masodon Dentist, Laurahird's Showcase, Dying Writers, ragged Edge, Showcase Press Poetry Journal*, (print issue) and *Strange Road*. In 2002, he was part of a spoken word/music CD Northport Celebrates Jack (a Kerouac tribute) featuring world famous musician David

Amram. He was also a student of Allen Ginsberg's for two years.

Greg Scharf
Greg Scharf used to live inside a garage in Los Angeles. He now lives above a garage but still drinks the same cheap off-brand vodka. Some of his other stuff can be found in recent issues of *Spent Meat*, *Underground Voices*, *My Favorite Bullet* and *Trespass*.

Mather Schneider
Mather Schneider is an unemployed cab driver living in Tucson with a Mexican girl. He has no college degree and has won no awards. He has a full length book coming out by Interior Noise Press.

Michael Shorb
Michael Shorb's work reflects an abiding interest in environmental issues, history, and the lyrical form, as well as a satirical focus on present day trends and events. His poems have appeared in over 100 magazines and anthologies, including *The Nation, The Sun, Michigan Quarterly Review, Queen's Quarterly, Poetry Salzburg Review, Commonweal, Religious Humanism, Shoofly, Rattle, Urthona*, and *European Judaism*, as well as such anthologies as *A Bell Ringing In An Empty Sky* (Mho and Mho Works), *To Be A Man* (Tarcher Press), *Names In A Jar: 100 American Poets* (Hood Press), *Underground Voices: Drugs, Guns, And Crazy Detectives*, and (upcoming) *The Great American Poetry Show 2*, and *On The Mekong* (short story) in *War Is All We Know* (Diverson Press).

John Sweet
John Sweet, 35 and counting, angry, bitter, etc etc, hiding in a pissant town in upstate New York, a believer in very little. A follower of the writings of J. Pollock and of the words of H. Frayne. Recent publications include the

chapbook *Enemy*, (www.pinkanarchkittypress.com), the full length collection *Human Cathedrals*, (www.ravennapress.com) and the electronic chapbook, *Silence in the House of Truths*.

Joseph Veronneau
Joseph Veronneau runs Scintillating Publications, publishers of fine chapbooks and the annual literary journal, AGUA. His own poems have appeared widely throughout the small press. He has 2 new chapbooks about to be released, one from Pudding House Press, the other from Propaganda Press.

Scott Wannberg
Scott Wannberg is the author of *Mr. Mumps* (Ouija Madness Press), *Electric Yes Indeed* (Shelf Life Press), *Amnesia Motel* (Dance of the Iguana Press), *Juice: the Musical!* (Rose of Sharon Press), *Equal Opportunity Sledgehammer* (Lummox Little Red Book Series), and *Nomads of Oblivion* (Lummox Little Red Book Series). His work is also included in *Twisted Cadillac*, a book about the Carma Bums (Sacred Beverage Press).

Lafayette Wattles
A graduate of Spalding University's MFA program, Lafayette Wattles was awarded a Ucross Foundation Fellowship. His poetry has appeared or is forthcoming in *Boxcar Poetry Review*, *Juked*, *FRIGG*, *13th Warrior Review*, *poeticdiversity*, *Big Toe Review*, *Not Just Air*, and *Word Riot*, among others. Two of Lafayette's poems were recently nominated for a Pushcart and for a Best of the Net Anthology award respectively.

Richard Wink
Richard Wink was born in 1984 in the 'Fine' City of Norwich. His poetry is routed in real life experiences and the complications of life, reflecting both the sacred

and the mundane. He has been published in *Concrete, Underground Window,* and *Aesthetica* magazine. His first chapbook of poetry published is out now titled *The Beehives* which is available via www.cogentpoetry.com

www.ingramcontent.com/pod-product-compliance
Lightning Source LLC
Chambersburg PA
CBHW020004050426
42450CB00005B/306